A FatCat Book

THE APOSTLES' CREED

For All God's Children

Art by
Natasha Kennedy

Text by
Ben Myers

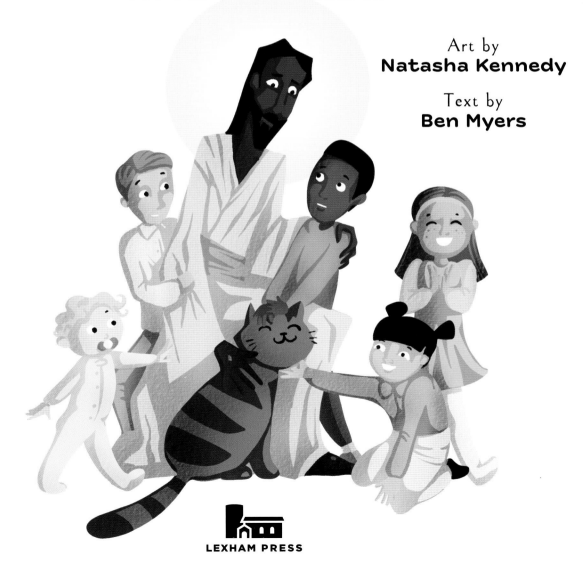

LEXHAM PRESS

ALMIGHTY AND EVERLASTING GOD

You sent your only Son to seek and to save the lost, saying through
him, "Let the little children come to me, and do not hinder them,
for to such belong the kingdom of God." It is not your will
that even one of these little ones should perish. Bless and
govern the children of your church by your Holy
Spirit, that they may grow in grace and in the
knowledge of your Word; protect and
defend them against all danger and
harm, giving your holy angels
charge over them; through
Jesus Christ, your
Son, our Lord.
AMEN.

What is FatCat?

How can anyone, no matter how young or old, grasp the message of the Bible? The church's answer has always been the catechism.

Maybe "catechism" sounds like a scary word. But it shouldn't! The catechism teaches us what the Bible teaches us: our faith. The church's catechism is the central texts of faith—the Apostles' Creed, the Ten Commandments, and the Lord's Prayer.

The catechism is "fat." It's bursting at the seams with meaning, challenge, and comfort. It's concise, but it's also deep. Most importantly, it should be familiar.

FatCat is our way of making the catechism approachable. And so this book has an actual fat cat hidden throughout. Search for him with your child as you enjoy this book together, and hide the words of the catechism in your heart.

"The unfolding of your words gives light;
it imparts understanding to the simple."
Psalm 119:130

I BELIEVE IN GOD,
THE FATHER ALMIGHTY

Who is God? What is God like?
Is God scary or unknown?

Jesus called God "Father."
He depends on God and comes from God.
Jesus lives in God forever with the Holy Spirit.
And Jesus has made me live with God too.
That's why I can call God "Father."

God is not a long way away.
I don't have to try hard to reach God.
God is right here with Jesus, right here with me.
Any time I look at Jesus, I see what God is like.
That's how good God is!

That's what I believe.

MAKER OF HEAVEN
AND EARTH

Where does the world come from?
Why am I here?

God made the light and the darkness.
God made the sky, the sea, and the land,
the plants and the trees,
the sun, the moon, and the stars,
the birds in the air and the fish in the sea.
God made animals and every living thing.
And then God made me.

God spoke, and it was done.

God wanted Jesus to have sisters and brothers,
That's why I'm here.
I'm here because God's life is big enough to share.

That's what I believe.

AND IN JESUS CHRIST,
HIS ONLY SON,
OUR LORD

Jesus has always been with God.
He is God's great Son forever.
He shares God's life in a special way.

But he wanted to share it with me too.
God's life is big enough to share!
So Jesus came from God.
He came to me.

Now Jesus has lots of brothers and sisters!
Whenever I am with his brothers and sisters,
I am with Jesus.
Whenever I am with Jesus, I am with God.

And God loves me as much as God loves Jesus.
That's how good God is!

That's what I believe.

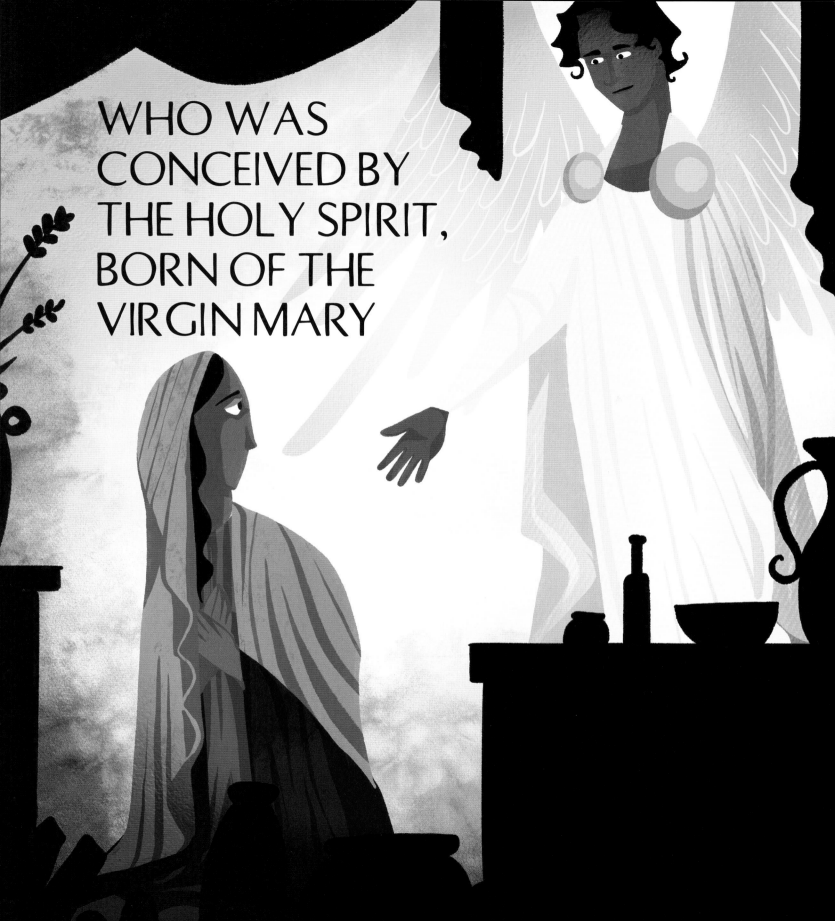

WHO WAS
CONCEIVED BY
THE HOLY SPIRIT,
BORN OF THE
VIRGIN MARY

Where did Jesus come from?
He is God's Son forever—but he has a mother too.
He was born like any baby.
He was always God and became human just like me.

I was lost, and he came into the world to find me.
I was alone, and he came into the world to meet me.

God's great Son became a little child.
Now I can be God's child too!
Now I can share the life that Jesus shares with God!

That's what I believe.

SUFFERED UNDER PONTIUS PILATE

What did Jesus want? He wanted us.
What did we do to him? We hurt him.
But why would anyone want to hurt God's Son?

Judas betrayed him.
Pilate judged him.
The crowd said, "Crucify him!"

Did he deserve it?
Did he ever do anything wrong?
Why did he suffer so much?

He suffered for us.
He suffered for me.

That's what I believe.

WAS CRUCIFIED, DIED, AND WAS BURIED

Jesus was treated like a criminal.
He was taken outside the city.
He was nailed to a wooden cross.
People mocked him.

He prayed to his Father: "Father, forgive them,
they don't know what they're doing."
And then he died.

Was he really dead or was he just pretending?

He really died. He did it freely.
He laid his life down as a gift.
His friends buried him and covered up the tomb.

Is this the end?
It's not the end! It's God's new beginning!

That's what I believe.

Where will I go when I die?
Where do all the dead go?
Wherever it is, Jesus went there too.

He went down as far as we had fallen.
He took death's keys to free the captives.
He overcame death with his life.

He took Eve and Adam, our first parents, by the hand
and made them his sister and brother.

When I die, Jesus meets me there and takes me by the hand.
He is God's strong Son, my strong Brother.

Is anything stronger than death?
Yes—Jesus!

That's what I believe.

ON THE THIRD DAY
HE ROSE AGAIN FROM THE DEAD

Why do I believe?

I believe because of something that really happened.
One day, in a garden long ago, a stone was rolled away.
The grave was empty.
The burial clothes were left behind.
"He is not here, he is risen!"

Because he is risen, the world is made new.
Because he is risen, every single life begins and ends with him.

This was a long time ago, but it really happened.
He defeated death: God's strong Son, my strong Brother,
the world's true Lord—and my Lord too.

On the third day, he rose again from the dead.
That's why I believe.

HE ASCENDED INTO HEAVEN

AND IS SEATED AT THE RIGHT HAND OF THE FATHER

Where is Jesus now?
Why can't I see him?
Is he still alive, still real?

Jesus is with God forever.
He's still human like me: he has scars in his hands.
But his life is God's life: he is strong with God's strength.

He sits with God and rules all things.
He speaks God's good news to me and to all nations.
He pours God's Holy Spirit into my life.
He makes God my Father.
He makes me part of his family.

That's what I believe.

HE WILL COME AGAIN TO JUDGE THE LIVING AND THE DEAD

Do I need to fear the future?
What if my life takes a wrong turn?
What if my dreams don't come true?
What if I make too many mistakes?

The one who died for me will be my judge.
The one who loves me will have the last word.
He has my future in his hands—
and those hands have scars for me.

Jesus, who sought me and found me, is my judge.

That is such good news!
And that's what I believe.

I BELIEVE IN THE HOLY SPIRIT

Is God far away?
Has Jesus left me all alone?
No! God is near—
very near!

Jesus lives forever with God in the Holy Spirit.
He shares God's life in a special way.
And Jesus sent the Holy Spirit to be with me.
Now I share God's life too and live in God.

Because of Jesus, I am in the Holy Spirit,
and so are all Jesus' brothers and sisters.
God is my family and my home.
I will never be far away from God—never again!

That's what I believe.

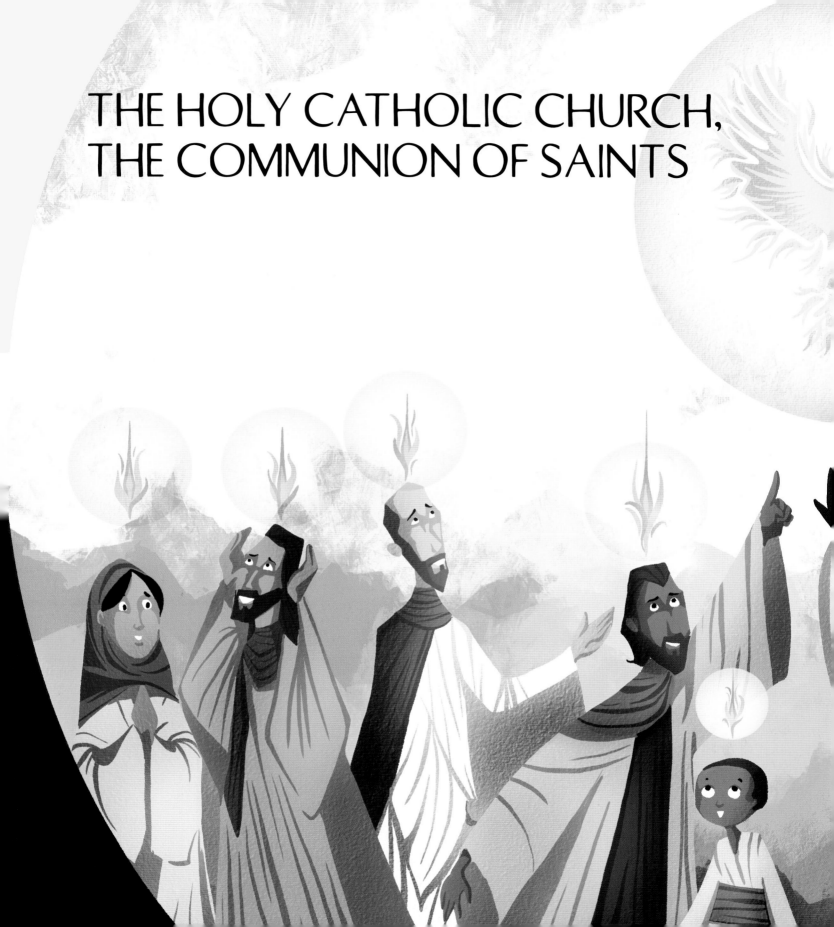

THE HOLY CATHOLIC CHURCH, THE COMMUNION OF SAINTS

Where is God in the world today?
God's life is shared with Jesus and
with all his brothers and sisters.
I can share God's life, and so can you!

God's family is so big—and it's always growing!
God's life is so big—and there's always more to share!
God's love for Jesus is so big—big enough to include everyone!

And I am part of it.
I will always be at home with God.
I will always be at home with Jesus,
and with his brothers and sisters in the Holy Spirit.

That's what I believe.

THE FORGIVENESS OF SINS

How did I get to be part of God's family?
Did I have to earn it?
Did I have to prove that I'm good enough for God?

God adopted me because God loves Jesus so much.
God wanted sisters and brothers for Jesus.
God welcomes me because of Jesus.
God forgives me because of Jesus.

But what if I make too many mistakes?
Will God ever reject me?
No! When God sees me, God sees Jesus.
God loves me as if I were Jesus,
as if I were God's own child—
which is exactly what I am!

That's what I believe.

THE RESURRECTION OF THE BODY

What happens when my life ends?
Will I be lost or forgotten?
Will I be far away from God?

When my life ends, I will be like Jesus
   on the third day.
God will raise me just as God raised Jesus.
I will still be me—but different!
I will be different—but still me!

I will be like Jesus, and I will see him.
I will be with Jesus' brothers and sisters.
We will live the new life that never dies:
the glorious freedom of the children of God.

That's what I believe.

AND THE LIFE EVERLASTING

Will Jesus ever stop sharing the Holy Spirit?
Will God ever stop loving Jesus
   and his sisters and brothers?

The life that Jesus shares is always new.
It never gets old. It never runs out. It never fails.

There will always be more of God's life to share.
Can I count all the sand on the beach?
Can I count all the stars in the sky?
That would be easier than counting all the good things
   that God has to share with me.

Life in God is so big and so full that it never ends.
And that life is mine to share right now!

That's what I believe.

AMEN

Who is God?
God is Father, Son, and Holy Spirit—
one God, one life, one Lord,
who is over all and through all and in all.
I know God's life because I live inside it.
I know God from the inside out.

God has one family,
always growing,
always sharing—
and because of Jesus, I'm a part of it!

That's why I say: Yes! Amen! I believe!

Families are little churches.

We pray together. We bring our sin and sadness, our joy and faith to the Lord our God. We read the Bible together. We hear Jesus' promises for us. And we forgive each other, because God, in Christ, has forgiven us.

The family is where catechesis (or instruction) in the basics of the Christian faith has taken place throughout the history of the church. This instruction has been built on what's called the "catechism"—that is, the Apostles' Creed, the Lord's Prayer, and the Ten Commandments. "Although I'm indeed an old doctor," Martin Luther said, "I never move on from the childish doctrine of the Ten Commandments and the Apostles' Creed and the Lord's Prayer. I still daily learn and pray them with my little Hans and my little Lena."

Catechesis can be as simple as praying the very words of the catechism. In worship, we sanctify our lives, days, and families by God's word and prayer (1 Timothy 4:5).

So here's a small service for family prayer for you and your children as you grow in the simple teaching of the Apostles' Creed.

This brief service of family prayer is designed to be prayed responsively. The leader reads the plain text; everyone reads the bold text. Even though your children might not be readers yet, they'll learn these words as you repeat them again and again each day. You could use it in the morning or evening—or anytime you and your children read this book.

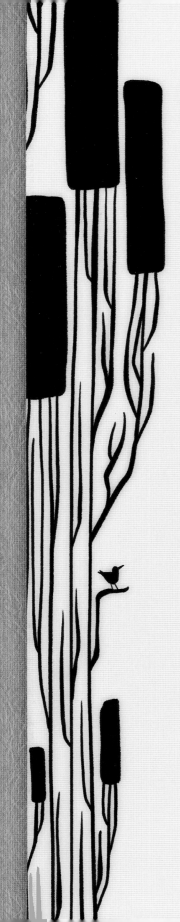

Family Prayer

In the name of the Father
and of the Son and of the Holy Spirit.
Amen.

The LORD is good,
his love endures forever.   Psalm 100:5

I hope in your word.
I am yours; save me.   Psalm 119:81, 94

The LORD is good,
his love endures forever.   Psalm 100:5

Blessed be the Lord,
who daily bears us up;
God is our salvation.   Psalm 68:19

The LORD is good,
his love endures forever.   Psalm 100:5

God has made us his people through our baptism into Christ. Living together in trust and hope, we confess our faith:

I believe in God, the Father almighty,
    maker of heaven and earth;
And in Jesus Christ, his only Son, our Lord;
    who was conceived by the Holy Spirit,
    born of the Virgin Mary,
    suffered under Pontius Pilate,
    was crucified, died, and was buried.
    He descended into hell.
    On the third day he rose again from the dead.
    He ascended into heaven,
    and is seated at the right hand of the Father.
    He will come again to judge the living and
    the dead.
I believe in the Holy Spirit,
    the holy catholic church,
    the communion of saints,
    the forgiveness of sins,
    the resurrection of the body,
    and the life everlasting.
Amen.

God is our loving Father.

He wants to hear our questions, fears, and joys.

Let us boldly offer our prayers for others and ourselves to God:

Parents, you might prompt your children's prayers by asking questions like:

What are you thankful for?
What are you afraid of?
What do you want to tell God?

You might also pray the words of the Bible, especially the Lord's Prayer, or the Apostles' Creed. Make these words your own!

Into your hands, O Lord, I commend myself, my body and soul, and all things. Let your holy angels be with me that the evil foe may have no power over me. Amen.

Let us bless the LORD.

Thanks be to God.

The grace of our Lord Jesus Christ and the love of God and the communion of the Holy Spirit be with us all.

2 Corinthians 13:14

Amen.

To Parents

It's daunting to illustrate the Apostles' Creed. The art needs to invite children into the creed and its awesome words. At the same time the art must be faithful to the words our God has spoken to us. To avoid slipping into speculation, God's word was set as the center and boundary of this book's art. As the psalmist says, "In your light we see light" (Psalm 36:9).

Our hope is that these images might spark your biblical imagination as you hear the words of the creed. At points, listening to the church's saints—for example, Martin Luther in his Small Catechism or John Chrysostom in his Paschal Homily—stirred up our own biblical imaginations. No doubt, you too will be encouraged and challenged by what the church's great cloud of witnesses has said about the Bible and the Apostles' Creed!

As an aid to your exploration of the Apostles' Creed, here are some of the passages that shaped and limited this book's art.

I believe in God, the Father almighty

Psalm 103	Matthew 3:13–17	1 Timothy 6:13–16
Revelation 4 (see Isaiah 6:1–3; Ezekiel 1)		

maker of heaven and earth

Psalm 104	Psalm 124:8	Genesis 1–2

And in Jesus Christ, his only Son, our Lord

Psalm 2	Matthew 3:13–17

who was conceived by the Holy Spirit, born of the Virgin Mary

Psalm 113	Matthew 1:26–38; 2:1–21

suffered under Pontius Pilate

Psalm 69	Matthew 26:36–27:26	Mark 2:1–12

was crucified, died, and was buried

Psalm 22	Matthew 27:27–66	Psalm 38:11
Luke 23:49	John 19:25	

He descended into *hell

Psalm 18	Ephesians 4:8–9	Philippians 2:9–11
1 Corinthians 15:54–55	1 Peter 3:18–22	Revelation 1:17–18

* Some English versions of the creed translate this line, "He descended to the dead."

on the third day he rose again from the dead

Psalm 16	Matthew 28:1–8	Mark 16:1–8
Luke 24:1–12	John 20:1–18	1 Corinthians 15:54–55

He ascended into heaven, and is seated at the right hand of the Father

Psalm 110	Luke 24:50–53	Acts 1:6–11
Psalm 47		

He will come again to judge the living and the dead

Psalm 72	Matthew 25:31–46	John 20:25–29
Luke 21:25–33		

I believe in the Holy Spirit

Psalm 33	Matthew 3:13–17

the holy *catholic church, the communion of saints

Psalm 1	Acts 2:1–4

* The phrase "catholic church" means all Christians throughout time and space who confess the Christian faith.

the forgiveness of sins

Psalm 130	John 8:1–11	Luke 1:77–79

the resurrection of the body

Psalm 49	Ezekiel 37:1–14
Malachi 4:2	1 Corinthians 15:23

and the life everlasting

Psalm 23
Revelation 21:10–25; 22:1–5
Ezekiel 41:17–20, 21–22;
    47:1–2, 12; 48:35
Genesis 2:8–14

The Apostles' Creed: For All God's Children
A FatCat Book

Copyright 2022 Lexham Press

Lexham Press, 1313 Commercial St., Bellingham, Washington 98225
LexhamPress.com

The prayer beginning "Almighty and everlasting God" is adapted from Collect 14, "For the Children of the Church," in *The Lutheran Hymnal* (Concordia, 1941), 103; quoting Luke 19:10; Luke 18:16; Matthew 18:14.

Printed in China.
ISBN 9781683595748
Library of Congress Control Number 2021939393

Series Editor: Todd Hains
Lexham Editorial: Abigail Stocker, Lindsay John Kennedy, Veronica Hains
Interior and Typeset Design: Natasha Kennedy
Cover Design: Lydia Dahl, Brittany Schrock
FatCat Icon: Micah Ellis
This book is typeset in FatCat, designed by Natasha Kennedy in 2021.